Good Business Isn't Rock

Book 1 of 6

Journeying

into the

Unknown!

STEPHEN PEAK VERNON BAILEY
CLIVE GOULDEN

Salisbury House
PUBLICATIONS

First published in Great Britain in 2005
by Salisbury House Publications
Salisbury House, 34 Salisbury Road, Burbage, Leicestershire LE10 2AR

A CIP catalogue record for this book is available from the British Library

ISBN 0-9545907-0-8

Printed in Great Britain for Salisbury House by:

Gartree Press Limited, Leicester

Cover design by:

Standout Design & Marketing

Good business isn't rocket science

Contents

Good business isn't rocket science

List of Tables

Introduction

Most business people believe that they "know" their business. To a large extent this is true. The power of the "gut feel" should never be underestimated and never ignored! But neither should it ever be relied upon as the sole source of assessment! One of the key factors identified in businesses that fail is an over dependence on intuition – "gut-feel"

Remember, the way you see things is not always the way others see them. You need to take time to think objectively about your business. Put that objectivity together with "gut feel" and you have a powerful recipe for success:

"Gut-feel" and "the cold-light-of-day."

The "gut feel" is all yours! What this book will do is give you a set of tools with which to make the "cold light of day" assessment. This set of tools is usually called "the strategic planning process" and that is what we will be going through - step by step. It is a simple process that is often shrouded in mystery by consultants and the like, but not here!

There is some argument as to whether strategic planning is a viable concept. However, as far as we are concerned:

"To fail to plan is to plan to fail."

Whilst strategic planning is not "rocket science" or some mystical power endowed only upon the chosen few, it does require some discipline to see it through and it often comes with some pain! Having said that, it will be an exciting, ultimately enjoyable and very rewarding journey through your business.

Drawing the Map

One of the most striking things we've discovered in years of research and working with companies is that most do not know where they are going, never mind how they are going to get there! They have an idea where they want to go, but don't really know, day by day, week by week, month by month, or sometimes even year by year if they are getting there. Neither is there normally any assessment as to the appropriateness of the destination. Originally, it may have been right but is it still?

To save yourself from journeying into the unknown you need to have a map. What we will do as we work together, through the process detailed in this book, is to draw your own strategic map for your department, business or organisation. The first thing we need to know is where you want to go, then we need to know where you are now and (in this exercise) how you got where you are now. Then we start to look at the options for getting where you want to go and how long the various options might take. Finally we choose your route and the way-markers that will tell you if you are on track. As a contingency, we may have a few alternative options up our sleeves as a hedge against adverse travelling conditions. So, let's kick-off by looking at the route ahead, in more detail, and see what ground we need to cover.

Chapter	Reason	Topics, material completed
1	This is the start of the journey where the corporate aim is decided. The aim acts as the impetus and gives focus to the whole journey.	Corporate aim
2	To set up our financial targets that will be included in the Gap analysis later on the journey.	Financial targets
3	To give an understanding on the importance of indicators and how they are used at corporate level.	Financial ratios
4	To set up our financial forecasts that will be included in the Gap analysis later on the journey	Financial forecasts
5	To evaluate the strategic significance of the finances over the next few years	Strategic financial route produced for budgeting etc.
6	To identify the strengths, weaknesses, opportunities and threats that the organisation is faced with during the next few years.	Major issues evaluated that will have an impact on the success of organisation.

Good business isn't rocket science

Chapter	Reason	Topics, material completed
7	To generate strategies from the Gap and SWOT analyses	Identifies issues that will need to be addressed if the targets are going to be achieved.
8	To evaluate the strategies and focus on key issues	Gives priority to core issues and details supporting ones.
9	Generate plan and check validity	Business plan finalised
10	Business plan produced and validated	Business plan accepted

1 *Where do we want to go?*

As we've already said, most of the time businesses are not very sure of where they want to go and neither are they very good at articulating it – which is really important if we want people to be able to work toward our desired destination. So, where does your business want to go (corporate aim) and how can you measure its progress (by Key Performance Indicators or KPI's)?

Corporate aim

The reason any commercial organisation exists is to provide financial returns to the owners. If you are an owner manager, I might hear you say: "Hang on! I'm not in it entirely for the money, I want a business to hand on to my children." Or, "I want long-term growth for my business, not just short-term profit." Or perhaps, "I want to reward my staff for their loyalty."
It must be clear here that there MUST be profit for the business to be handed on, or to fund growth, or to reward staff for their loyalty. If these are your objectives they can help define the level of financial performance required. Even in most not-for-profit organisations you need to generate financial surpluses to ensure survival.

So, where do you want your business to go; what do you want it to achieve?
Here are some examples of what individuals want out from their organisations during the next few years:

- To improve it's financial performance and generate increasing amounts of profit;
- To increase the level of quality assurance through staff training and culture changes so that it moves towards a right first time culture;
- To continue to increase its range of capabilities and processing capacity, whilst steadily raising its profile as a specialist out-sourcing provider;
- To become more recognised as a development company (solving production problems) rather than merely a contractor without any intellectual property;

Good business isn't rocket science

- To change its priorities in order to get a better balance of short term operational and longer term strategic management time
- To ensure that the organisation continues to develop to become recognised as a world class manufacturing facility;
- To develop a more formalised management structure so that all managers feel they can contribute to decision making process.

Now it's your turn!
But don't think about the final wording yet, in the box below just write down exactly why your business exists and what you want your business to achieve, being as specific as you can.

Go for it:……..

Why does the business exist?

What do you want your business to achieve?

You now need to develop the above thoughts into a concise statement that will be robust enough for criticism and still provide the organisation's staff with a focus for the next few years.

If you are going to publish your corporate aim in any way e.g. to your staff or in marketing material, you may need to couch it in different terms. For instance: "to have a business worth £X pounds in five years so I can retire and/or hand over to my children" might also be expressed as: "to generate X% net profit before tax to our parent company" or "To return Y% Return On Sales to our shareholders".

Good business isn't rocket science

Here is Ford's corporate aim to use as an example. But bear in mind that all corporate aims are different because they all reflect the varied types, sizes and cultures of the organisations they represent.

> *"The Company is a worldwide leader in automotive and automotive-related products and services as well as in newer industries such as aerospace, communications and financial services. Our mission is to improve continually our products and services to meet our customers' needs, allowing us to prosper as a business and to provide a reasonable return for our stockholders, the owners of our business."*

Now let's see your corporate aim written in the box below. However, bear in mind that you may have to revisit it after completing the exercises further on in the book as you may well be finding out facts that you may need to give some consideration to in the corporate aim.

Corporate aim:

2   *What will it take to get there?*

Targets

Now we have established the reason your business exists and what you want from it let's move on to put some financial targets against the objectives.

Targets are what you "want" to happen, as opposed to forecasts, which are what you "expect" to happen (based on what you've already achieved and taking into account any known future developments). If you only use forecasts the business is managing you! Targets enable you to manage the business to meet your objectives.

At this stage we need to establish two preliminary targets that we will review later in the light of further information. The first is "Acceptable Target (AT)" which is the lowest performance you will accept before closing the business. The second is "Satisfactory Target (ST)" and this, as its name suggests, is satisfactory financial performance.

The next thing to decide is what measure you are going to use for your targeting. Our recommendation is always (with few exceptions) to include Profit (before tax & interest) but you may decide to include Return on Capital Employed (ROCE) or even Sales. As we have already said, you need profit to fund whatever you want to do with the business. A lack of retained profit and the often resultant over-gearing (borrowing too much money) are major factors in 70% of business failures. If you decide to include ROCE then AT should not be less than the cost of borrowing.

These targets should be developed for the current year and for a minimum of the next four years. In the example overleaf (Table 1) and Table 2 on the following page (for you to fill in) we have included a number of suggested target measures. You almost certainly won't want to use all of them but they will make you think as you pick and choose those that seem appropriate to you and fill in the table. If you are not used to doing this sort of thing don't worry, nobody is marking you out of ten. If you are not sure what some of the ratios mean or how to calculate them again, don't worry. All will be explained later and you can come back to them. Just take a stab at what you think; there will be plenty of time for re-evaluation later in the process.

Good business isn't rocket science

Table 1. Everyorg Ltd example of targets

Example of the information we want you to provide. This is repeated for you, with formulae, in Table 2.

	Current	1	2	3	4	5
1. Planning Year						
2. Calendar Year						
3. Turnover increased by 10% (£) All £'s are in thousands, i.e. £'000's.	9,887	10,876	11,964	13,160	14,476	
4. Acceptable shareholder Return (£) the minimum net profit that will be accepted by the shareholders	65	70	75	80	85	
5. Investment required to 'stand still' (£) the money that needs to be spent to maintain existing levels of service, usually replacement costs etc, over and above labour and materials costs	10	11	12	13	14	
6. AT Profit (£)	75	81	87	93	99	
7. AT ROS %	0.8	0.7	0.7	0.7	0.7	
8. Satisfactory shareholder Return (£) the level of net profit that will be acceptable to the shareholders	1,977	2,175	2,393	2,632	2,895	
9. Investment required for growth (£) the money that needs to be spent to meet the growth demands of the business, e.g. capital expenditure for new equipment to increase productivity	15	25	26	35	40	
10. Borrowings to fund investment (£) the money that will need to be spent to realise growth, e.g. loans, interest etc.	0	2	2	4	5	
11. ST Profit (£)	1,992	2,202	2,421	2,671	2,940	
12. ST ROS %	20.2	20.2	20.2	20.3	20.3	
1. Capital employed to 'stand still' (£) Present Total Assets minus Total Liabilities with necessary increases	3,190	3,403	3,7647	4,205	4,584	
14. AT ROCE %	2.4	2.4	2.3	2.2	2.2	
2. Capital employed for growth (£) Present Total Assets minus Total Liabilities with increases to reflect expected growth	3,315	3,452	3,876	4,426	4,782	
16. ST ROCE %	60.1	63.8	62.5	60.3	61.5	

Good business isn't rocket science

Table 2. Targets

	Formula	Current	1	2	3	4	5
1. Planning Year							
2. Calendar Year							
3. Turnover (£)[1]							
4. Acceptable shareholder Return. (£)							
5. Investment required to 'stand still'. (£)							
6. AT Profit (£)	4 + 5						
7. AT ROS %	(6/3)*100						
8. Satisfactory shareholder Return. (£)							
9. Investment required for growth. (£)							
10. Borrowings to fund investment. (£)							
11. ST Profit (£)	7 + 8 + 9						
12. ST ROS %	(11/3)*100						
13. Capital employed to 'stand still'. (£)							
14. AT ROCE %	(6/13)*100						
15. Capital employed for growth. (£)							
16. ST ROCE %	(11/15)*100						

Capital Employed
The amount of 'capital employed' within the company is the Total Assets minus the Total Liabilities. This figure is equal to the ordinary and preference share capital, all reserves and the profit and loss account balances.

---

[1] (£) = £'000's

Good business isn't rocket science

Once you have completed as much of Table 2 as you see fit you need to make a graph of your targets (this will be used later on with your forecasts). It really does help to make these things more visual and it will also be useful in making comparisons later on. We've included a page of graph paper as Table 4, but if you can use a computer spreadsheet (we've used Microsoft Excel in the example below) all the better.

Table 3.   Everyorg Ltd example of target graph

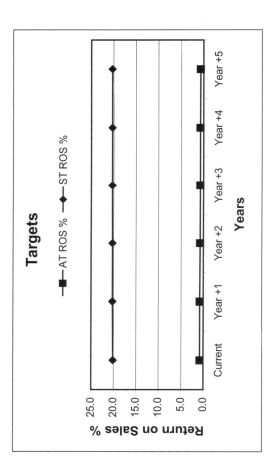

Once you have completed the above tasks and if you are typical of the businesses we have researched or worked with, you will have already created a clearer and more defined picture of where you want to be than ever before. You will also have found it an invigorating and interesting exercise and will be armed with valuable and powerful information.

Good business isn't rocket science

Table 4.   Graph for Targets

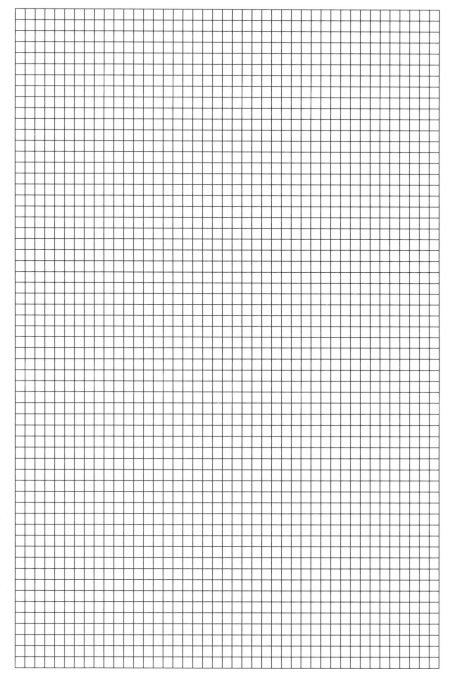

3 *Crunching the numbers*

The next stage in the Strategic Planning Process we need to get to grips with is that of having a good understanding of the performance of our business. Our favoured approach is to look at the performance over the past five years. This is incredibly powerful in helping us understand how we got where we are and what the issues were on the way. If we are to forecast ahead we must know what happened in the past. Managing a business on the basis of past financial performance alone is like driving a car using only the rear view mirror, we know what the traffic conditions are behind us, but what are they like on our journey ahead? Just as good drivers use the rear view mirror as one of a number of sources of information about the road, so this review will be one of a number of sources of information used to assess the position of your business.

There are many different "numbers" that we could look at to make an assessment of performance but here we will concentrate on financial performance. You have already given some thought to this in the previous section, but now we will develop those thoughts a little further as we look at some key ratios for each of the past five years. But before we get into that let's have a quick look at some ratios and what they mean.

There are a vast array of ratios that have been developed for specialist analysis, the few simple ratios that we will look at, when put together, give a good indication of how a business has performed. They have been worked out for you in the Everyorg examples in Tables 5, 7 and 9 and are broken down into:

- Profitability ratios
- Capital ratios, and
- Management ratios, as shown below.

3.1 Profitability ratios

Return on sales (ROS) - can be expressed as £'s or as a %, but more useful as a %.

It is easy to get misled into believing a business is doing well because turnover (sales) is increasing. Many people believe that "if we can increase turnover we will make more money" but this is not necessarily true! We must look at the "quality" of our turnover, the profitability.

$$\frac{\text{Profit before tax \& interest (Net Profit)}}{\text{Sales (Turnover)}}$$

A reducing trend may indicate for example that competition is driving down prices or that there is an increasing cost base within the business.

3.2 Capital ratios

These ratios tell us how well the capital invested in the business has been working. In general, the higher these ratios are the better, so increasing trends are to be welcomed. However, if buildings and equipment are leased and thus "off balance sheet" we may get an unduly optimistic view. Positive trends may also be pointing to low investment storing up problems for the future.

Return on capital employed (ROCE)

$$\frac{\text{Profit before tax \& interest}}{\text{Capital employed}}$$

Asset utilisation

$$\frac{\text{Turnover}}{\text{Capital employed}}$$

3.3 Management ratios

Stock turns

(where applicable)
Within a manufacturing environment stock turn is an important measure of the efficiency of production control and inventory management. A ratio of four equates to three months worth of stock and a ratio of twelve to one months worth of stock. The lower the ratio the more cash and facilities are tied up in stock.

$$\frac{\text{Turnover}}{\text{Stock}}$$

Debtor days

Excessive debtor days could indicate poor financial management in terms of credit control or perhaps quality of invoicing. It could also point to dissatisfaction within the customer base or particular problems in a particular sector.

$$\frac{\text{Debtors x 365}}{\text{Turnover}}$$

Creditor days

Excessive creditor days could indicate poor financial management in terms of cash flow control and could damage the business by alienating suppliers.

$$\frac{\text{Creditors x 365}}{\text{Turnover}}$$

Sales per employee

Sales per employee will vary according to the nature of the business and across different industries. It is a valuable trend to plot within a business as for example, reducing sales per employee could indicate reducing efficiency and over staffing.

$$\frac{\text{Turnover}}{\text{Number of employees}}$$

Good business isn't rocket science

Most of the content of Tables 5 & 7, apart from "stock", should be relevant to every type of business.

Now you have had a look at some ratios, choose which seem appropriate and complete Table 6 and Table 8 with its graph, Table 10, on the following pages. Remember, no-one is looking over your shoulder, just have a go!

When you have done that, decide which are the most important to you and introduce them into your monthly statistics.

Good business isn't rocket science

Table 5.   Everyorg Ltd example of five year performance review – Profitability and Capital ratios

	Formula	Year -5	Year -4	Year -3	Year -2	Year -1
1. Planning Year						
2. Calendar Year						
3. Turnover (£'000's)		5,696	5,867	7,529	8,245	8,989
4. Net Profit (£) (before tax and interest)		600	687	1,323	1,642	2,073
5. Inflation*	@ 4% p.a.	100	104	108	112	117
6. Real turnover growth (£)	(3*(100/5)	5,696	5,641	6,961	7,330	7,683
7. Real profit growth (£)	(4*(100/5)	600	661	1,223	1,460	1,772
8. Return on sales (%)	(7/6)*100	10.5	11.7	17.6	19.9	23.1
9. Capital employed (£)	Total Assets minus Total Liabilities	3,190	3,403	3,764	4,205	4,584
10. Real growth of capital employed (£)	(9*(100/5)	3,190	3,272	3,480	3,738	3,919
11. Real Return on capital employed (%)	(7/9)*100	18.8	20.2	35.1	39.1	45.2
12. Real Asset utilisation	(6/10)*100	1.8	1.7	2.0	2.0	2.0

*Put in actual inflation figures and apply to 6, 7, & 10.

Now its your turn to fill in the boxes with your own information! Use Table 4 on the next page.

Good business isn't rocket science

Table 6.   Your five year performance review – Profitability and Capital ratios

	Formula	Year -5	Year -4	Year -3	Year -2	Year -1
1. Planning Year						
2. Calendar Year						
3. Turnover (£'000's)						
4. Net Profit (£) (before tax and interest)						
5. Inflation*	@ % p.a.	100				
6. Real turnover growth (£)	(3*(100/5)					
7. Real profit growth (£)	(4*(100/5)					
8. Return on sales (%)	(7/6)*100					
9. Capital employed (£)	Total Assets minus Total Liabilities					
10. Real growth of capital employed (£)	(9*(100/5)					
11. Return on capital employed (%)	(7/9)*100					
12. Real Asset utilisation	(6/10)*100					

*Put in actual inflation figures and apply to 6, 7, & 10.

Good business isn't rocket science

Table 7. Everyorg Ltd example: Five year performance review – Management ratios

	Formula	Year -5	Year -4	Year -3	Year -2	Year -1
1. Planning Year						
2. Calendar Year						
3. Real Turnover (£'000's)		5,696	5,641	6,961	7,330	7,683
4. Stock (£)		1,256	1,345	1,453	1,512	1,485
5. Stock turns	$\frac{Turnover}{Stock}$	4.5	4.2	4.8	4.9	5.2
6. Debtors (£)		1,124	1,354	1,342	1,307	1,284
7. Debtor days	$\frac{Debtors \times 365}{Turnover}$	72	88	70	65	61
8. Creditors (£)		1,184	1,245	1,442	1,423	1,456
9. Creditor days	$\frac{Creditors \times 365}{Turnover}$	76	81	76	71	69
10. Number of employees		83	85	95	96	97
11. Sales per employee	$\frac{Turnover}{No.\ of\ employees}$	68.6	66.4	73.3	76.4	79.2

Good business isn't rocket science

Table 8. Your five year performance review – Management ratios

Now its your turn again to fill in the boxes and construct a graph with your own information!

	Formula	Year -5	Year -4	Year -3	Year -2	Year -1
1. Planning Year						
2. Calendar Year						
3. Real Turnover (£'000's)						
4. Stock (£)						
5. Stock turns	$\frac{Turnover}{Stock}$					
6. Debtors (£)						
7. Debtor days	$\frac{Debtors \times 365}{Turnover}$					
8. Creditors (£)						
9. Creditor days	$\frac{Creditors \times 365}{Turnover}$					
10. Number of employees						
11. Sales per employee	$\frac{Turnover}{No. \ of \ employees}$					

Good business isn't rocket science

Table 9. Graph of Profitability, Capital and Management ratios

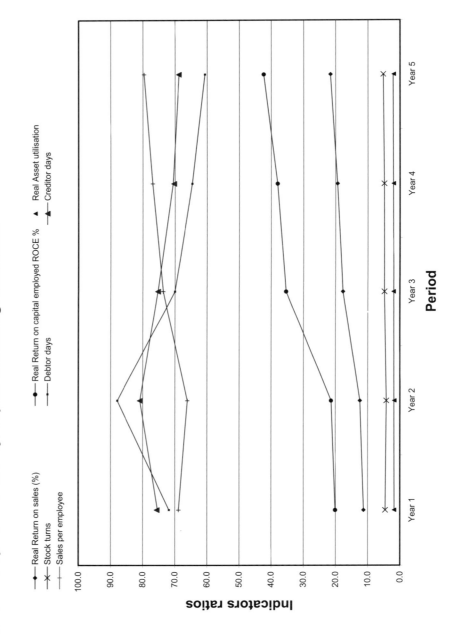

Good business isn't rocket science

Table 10.   Your graph of Profitability, Capital and Management ratios

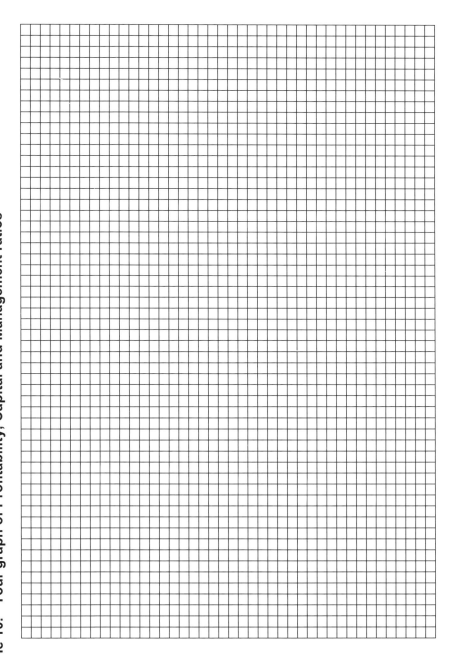

Good business isn't rocket science

You have now developed information on where you want to be and have gathered a lot of data on how you got where you are. We now want to turn that data into information by applying some thought to it. Take a look at Table 11 below, then summarise the trends from the graphs you created and give some thought to why they are as they are. Be as objective and as honest with yourself as you can and perhaps ask other people for their opinion. The accuracy of the information you gather here is of great importance as we begin to use it to plan for the future. If you don't think the indicators we have suggested are the most important to you – change them, its your map!

Table 11. Everyorg Ltd example of five year performance record overview

Financial health indicators	Summary of trends	Main explanation
1. Return on sales (%)	Shows gradual increase with improvement from year 2 to 3.	Climate fostered continual growth but new equipment introduced gave increased rates of return from year 3.
2. Return on capital employed (%)	Mirrors ROS above but shows a higher increase from year 2 to 3.	Shows higher return from year 2 to 3 compared to ROS as capital employed did not rise significantly compared to higher net profit realised.
3. Asset utilisation	Looks constant on the graph, owing to the scale but rose from year 2 to year 3.	Demonstrates more efficient use of assets with an increase in turnover from year 3.
4. Stock turns	Graph scale does not show up stock inefficiency in year 2 and its subsequent continued recovery.	Shows an improvement in the performance of stock management from a downturn in year 2.
5. Debtor days	Increase in days shows lack of control that has been better managed after year 2.	Better system controls were available after year 2 when the number of debtor days had to be below the number of creditor days for effective cash flow management.
6. Creditor days	Shows out of control situation in year 2.	Lower figure than debtor days means we were paying before we got the money in. This changed and became better managed.
7. Sales per employee	Gradual increase in sales per employee after year 2.	Demonstrates better staff efficiency and use of resources.

22

Good business isn't rocket science

Now its your turn to complete the trend summary of ratios and their meanings for your organisation.

Table 12. Five year performance record overview

Financial health indicators	Summary of trends	Main explanation
1. Return on sales (%)		
2. Return on capital employed (%)		
3. Asset utilisation		
4. Stock turns		
5. Debtor days		
6. Creditor days		
7. Sales per employee		

If this is running true to form you have already found out many interesting things about your business that you did not appreciate before. You have also created two parts of the map, where you want to be and where you are now. Let's get onto the next part of the map and look at where the journey is currently taking us.

4 Checking the rear view mirror!

In this section we are going to look at the financial forecasts for your business. Why forecasts and targets? Having decided what we want from the business (see targets), we now look at what we should expect from the organisation(forecasts). If the forecasts exceed our targets then we will be in a strong position and will probably be very pleased! If forecasts equal targets we will still need to be careful but may be satisfied. However, if our forecasts are less than our targets then the ugly truth has come to light and action of some sort is required!

Forecasting

To create these forecasts we will need to collect and analyse some data. When we have done this we will require two forecasts, High Forecast (HF) – what would happen if a few things went well and Low Forecast (LF) – what would happen if a few things did not go so well. When forecasting we look at future trends based on historical data, current information, and any future factors that can be identified. In doing this we assume that the organisation continues to be managed in the same way as it is now, but that the environment around it will change.

So, it's on with the show again by reviewing the next few steps in the process. It may be useful if you remember the next page (25) so that you can come back to check where you are amongst the numerous pages of analysis. These pages cover the following steps and are numbered as shown here.

Good business isn't rocket science

These steps are:

Preparation of forecasting information

1.   Identify your main products or services.
2.   Determine the performance of each main product/service over the last five years.
3.   Summarise the performances.

That's most of the groundwork done so let's start the forecasting.

Developing the forecasts

1.   Developing and summarising the Low Forecasts.
2.   Developing and summarising the High Forecasts.
3.   Graphing the forecasts.

Now we'll take a look at these sections in turn.

Good business isn't rocket science

Preparation of forecasting information

1.   Identify your main products or services.

To do this we need to look at what has been happening over the last five years and what is happening currently.

We have provided an example for you from our scenario organisation Everyorg Ltd. In the example we write up a brief history of the products/services that we have selected as being the most important of our portfolio. To decide which are the most important we use the 80/20 principle (where 80% of your turnover comes from 20% of your range of items) for this prioritisation process.

In Everyorg we have four main items but, of course a real organisation may have more, although we try to work with no more than five or six if possible. Generic groups may be selected, it all depends on your own organisation.

After the brief products/services history we identify any areas that may affect our future operations. You will notice from our Everyorg example that most of the considerations raised are external ones that impact on the organisation.

Once you've gone through Everyorg's example its time to have a go yourself. For each product or service you need to consider, enter the details in the appropriate boxes in Table 14 on page 31.

See the notes at the top of the table.

Good business isn't rocket science

Table 13. Everyorg Ltd's main products/services (termed items)

Products/Service	Brief History	Factors Affecting Future
Item A	Successful item introduced some 8 years ago. Ran into problems 4 years ago when old equipment was being replaced and during the transition period output could not keep up with demand. In spite of this hiccup profitability has increased until it is the main item in the portfolio. Work on staff productivity has brought good gains and supplier agreements have been in place for some years allowing better planning and control.	Product life cycle is still strong but competitors are gradually catching up and this may limit price increases. Market research leads us to believe that volumes should maintain growth rate of at least 5% and prices should still be able to increase by 6% for the foreseeable future owing to improvements that more satisfy customer demands and reduce competition.
Item B	Second most important item after A with continuous steady sales during the past 5 years. Similar to A in that productivity improvements have been achieved and working with suppliers has brought efficiencies. Level of item's net profit very acceptable. There is some evidence that sales have been limited owing to price rises in excess of the cost of living.	Market research leads us to believe that sales increases of at least 6% are possible if prices are restricted to the cost of living (3%) for the foreseeable future. Negotiations with suppliers to limit price increases may be successful as in Item A and so anticipate a slight saving in materials costs of at least 1%. If this strategy is successful then the resulting net profit for this item will be significant.
Item C	This has been another good item over the years with sound sales increases in excess of 6% year on year. In spite of continued increases in staff and materials costs, profitability has shown a significant rise owing to price increases complementing increased sales.	Difficult to see this item performing badly in this climate which looks to be quite settled. Costs will still need to increase to maintain skilled labour and quality materials but prices increases on this item do not appear to be a problem.
Item D	Dramatic increases in sales over the past 5 years have brought this item into second turnover and net profitability position. This item is now responsible for over a third of the turnover and just under a third of the net profit	Market evidence suggests that sales levels will continue to rise in line with the good results of previous years. Some work is being done with suppliers that should keep materials increases in line with the cost of living and enhance profitability.

27

Good business isn't rocket science

Table 14. Factors affecting your organisation's future

This analysis should be limited to your main groups. More than four, for example, would increase the workload but not the usefulness. So we try to limit our analysis from three to five. When considering the factors effecting the future you should include what is, or might happen in terms of: new technologies and materials, new products and changing customer/ market needs. Try to be as broad ranging in your considerations as possible and gather information as appropriate, e.g. from staff, competitors and the trade press.

Products/Service	Brief History	Factors Affecting Future

2. Determine the performance of each main product/service over the last five years.

This may seem tedious but hang in there, it will pay dividends. It is all adding up to the most detailed and powerful picture of your business that you have ever had. To help you we've provided Everyorg's examples of its main four items performance during the past five years on the following pages (in our context an item is a product or service), i.e.

Table 15.   Example from Everyorg Ltd of product / service history Item A

on page 30

Table 16.   Example from Everyorg Ltd of product / service history Item B

on page 31

Table 17.   Example from Everyorg Ltd of product / service history Item C

on page 32

Table 18.   Example from Everyorg Ltd of product / service history Item D

on page 33

Now its time for you to analyse your own information in Table 19 which appears after the Everyorg examples on page 34.

Table 19 looks at the sales revenue, numbers sold, the unit price, costs of labour and materials, and any other direct costs. Complete as many Table 19's as necessary (the same as the number of products/services you have entered in Table 14).

Good business isn't rocket science

Table 15. Example from Everyorg Ltd of product / service history   Item A

We now have to record some history before getting onto the forecasts and we do this by filling in the first half (left to right) of the table below for each of the Items we selected in the previous table - Factors affecting the future. We need to see how they have performed during the previous 5 years before we are able to forecast any results for them.

Product/Service: ....Item A.........

	Planning Year	-5	-4	-3	-2	-1	Current year	1	2	3	4	5
	Calendar Year											
1	Sales Revenue (£'000's)	2,124	2,111	2,617	2,912	3,169						
2	Volume (units)	187,256	175,643	205,414	215,613	221,357						
3	Selling Price/unit (£) (1÷2)	11.34	12.02	12.74	13.51	14.32						
4	Direct cost of labour (£'000's)	513	501	498	543	580						
5	Direct cost of material (£'000's)	910	896	1,101	1,213	1,308						
6	Other direct Costs (£'000's)	0	0	0	0	0						
7	Total direct Costs (£'000's) (4+5+6)	1,423	1,397	1,598	1,756	1,888						
8	Contribution (£'000's) (1-7)	701	714	1,019	1,156	1,281						
9	Overheads (£'000's)											
10	Profit (£'000's) (8-9)											

Good business isn't rocket science

Table 16.   Example from Everyorg Ltd of product / service history   Item B

Product/Service: ....Item B.............

	Planning Year	-5	-4	-3	-2	-1	Current year	1	2	3	4	5
	Calendar Year											
1	Sales Revenue (£'000's)	1,251	1,263	1,342	1,412	1,491						
2	Volume (units)	98,146	94,371	95,442	95,644	96,223						
3	Selling Price/unit (£) (1÷2)	12.75	13.39	14.06	14.76	15.50						
4	Direct cost of labour (£'000's)	380	380	384	400	419						
5	Direct cost of material (£'000's)	328	331	352	352	372						
6	Other direct Costs (£'000's)	0	0	0	0	0						
7	Total direct Costs (£'000's) (4+5+6)	708	711	736	753	791						
8	Contribution (£'000's) (1-7)	543	552	606	659	700						
9	Overheads (£'000's)											
10	Profit (£'000's) (8-9)											

Good business isn't rocket science

Table 17. Example from Everyorg Ltd of product / service history   Item C

Product/Service: ....Item C.............

	Planning Year / Calendar Year	-5	-4	-3	-2	-1	Current year	1	2	3	4	5
1	Sales Revenue (£'000's)	428	464	505	558	616						
2	Volume (units)	46,762	47,851	49,102	51,236	53,344						
3	Selling Price/unit (£) (1÷2)	9.15	9.70	10.28	10.90	11.55						
4	Direct cost of labour (£'000's)	175	186	199	216	234						
5	Direct cost of material (£'000's)	111	119	128	140	153						
6	Other direct Costs (£'000's)	0	0	0	0	0						
7	Total direct Costs (£'000's) (4+5+6)	285	305	327	356	387						
8	Contribution (£'000's) (1-7)	143	159	178	202	229						
9	Overheads (£'000's)											
10	Profit (£'000's) (8-9)											

Good business isn't rocket science

Table 18. Example from Everyorg Ltd of product / service history   Item D

Product/Service: ....Item D.................

	Planning Year	-5	-4	-3	-2	-1	Current year	1	2	3	4	5
	Calendar Year											
1	Sales Revenue (£'000's)	1,547	1,672	2,669	2,946	3,201						
2	Volume (units)	312,456	318,564	479,826	499,627	512,234						
3	Selling Price/unit (£) (1÷2)	4.95	5.25	5.56	5.90	6.25						
4	Direct cost of labour (£'000's)	709	752	1,178	1,276	1,360						
5	Direct cost of material (£'000's)	412	442	698	764	822						
6	Other direct Costs (£'000's)	0	0	0	0	0						
7	Total direct Costs (£'000's) (4+5+6)	1,121	1,194	1,876	2,040	2,182						
8	Contribution (£'000's) (1-7)	426	478	793	906	1,019						
9	Overheads (£'000's)											
10	Profit (£'000's) (8-9)											

Good business isn't rocket science

Table 19.   Your organisation's product/service history

Now let's see if you can fill in the table with your own information. Work on the items, products or services you have decided on in Table 14 and then provide copies of this form for each and enter your own information as we have done in the Everyorg Ltd examples on the previous pages.

Product/Service: ....

Planning Year	-5	-4	-3	-2	-1	Current year	1	2	3	4	5
Calendar Year											
1	Sales Revenue (£'000's)											
2	Volume (units)											
3	Selling Price/unit (£) (1÷2)											
4	Direct cost of labour (£'000's)											
5	Direct cost of material (£'000's)											
6	Other direct Costs (£'000's)											
7	Total direct Costs (£'000's) (4+5+6)											
8	Contribution (£'000's) (1-7)											
9	Overheads (£'000's)											
10	Profit (£'000's) (8-9)											

34

Good business isn't rocket science

3. Summarise the performances.

Having analysed our main items its time to bring them together so that we can eventually draw some conclusions on the overall picture of the organisation's performance.

We've done this in Everyorg's example in Table 20 below. What you have to do is to bring your analysis from the sheets you've filled in Table 19 format and put the information in Table 21 on the next page.

You're doing a great job, keep going! We're almost at the forecasting itself.

Table 20. Example from Everyorg Ltd of product/service histories summary

	Planning Year	-5	-4	-3	-2	-1	Current year	1	2	3	4	5
	Calendar Year											
	Product / service	£'000's										
1	Item A	Contribution	701	714	1,019	1,156	1,281						
2	Item B	Contribution	543	552	606	659	700						
3	Item C	Contribution	143	159	178	202	229						
4	Item D	Contribution	426	478	793	906	1,019						
5	Other items	Contribution	81	89	103	116	131						
6		Total/year	1,894	1,994	2,753	3,153	3,589						
7		Overheads (including fixed labour)	1,293	1,307	1,430	1,511	1,516						
8		Profit	600	687	1,323	1,642	2,073						

Good business isn't rocket science

Table 21. Your organisation's product/service history summary

Now transfer your information from Table 19 to the table below and complete rows 5 to 8.

	Planning Year		-5	-4	-3	-2	-1	Current year	1	2	3	4	5
	Calendar Year												
	Product / service	£'000's											
1	Item A	Contribution											
2	Item B	Contribution											
3	Item C	Contribution											
4	Item D	Contribution											
5	Other items	Contribution											
6		Total/year											
7		Overheads (including fixed labour)											
8		Profit											

Developing the forecasts

Having completed the historical part of the number crunching we go on to the forecasting itself. There are two different forecasts we determine from our previous history analysis work in Tables 19 (+more) and 21:

- A Low or pessimistic Forecast (LF), and

- A High or optimistic Forecast (HF).

Once these have been decided we summarise them to provide two pictures of possible outcomes, a desirable one and a poor one.

1. Developing and summarising the Low Forecasts
As the title suggests this type of forecast takes the poorest view from your analysis of issues that will affect the future of your organisation.

The next pages are devoted to this analysis and are set out as follows:

Table 22.   Everyorg Ltd's Low Forecast of Item A

Table 23.   Everyorg Ltd's Low Forecast of Item B

Table 24.   Everyorg Ltd's Low Forecast of Item C

Table 25.   Everyorg Ltd's Low Forecast of Item D

Table 26.   Everyorg Ltd's Low Forecast Summary.

Table 27.   for your own Low Forecast figures (as many as you need), and

Table 28.   for your Low Forecast Summary.

Good business isn't rocket science

Table 22. Example from Everyorg Ltd of product / service Low Forecast   Item A
Product/Service: ....Item A......Low Forecast

	Planning Year	-5	-4	-3	-2	-1	Current year	1	2	3	4	5
	Calendar Year											
1	Sales Revenue (£'000's)	2,124	2,111	2,617	2,912	3,169	3,324	3,424	3,527	3,634	3,743	3,856
2	Volume (units)	187,256	175,643	205,414	215,613	221,357	227,611	229,887	232,186	234,507	236,852	239,221
3	Selling Price/unit (£) (1÷2)	11.34	12.02	12.74	13.51	14.32	14.60	14.89	15.19	15.50	15.81	16.12
4	Direct cost of labour (£'000's)	513	501	498	543	580	590	614	639	664	691	719
5	Direct cost of material (£'000's)	910	896	1,101	1,213	1,308	1,219	1,231	1,244	1,319	1,332	1,345
6	Other direct Costs (£'000's)	0	0	0	0	0	0	0	0	0	0	0
7	Total direct Costs (£'000's) (4+5+6)	1,423	1,397	1,598	1,756	1,888	1,810	1,846	1,883	1,984	2,024	2,065
8	Contribution (£'000's) (1-7)	701	714	1,019	1,156	1,281	1,513	1,578	1,644	1,649	1,719	1,791
9	Overheads (£'000's)											
10	Profit (£'000's) (8-9)											

Good business isn't rocket science

Table 23. Example from Everyorg Ltd of product / service Low Forecast   Item B

Product/Service: ....Item B...Low Forecast

	Planning Year	-5	-4	-3	-2	-1	Current year	1	2	3	4	5
	Calendar Year											
1	Sales Revenue (£'000's)	1,251	1,263	1,342	1,412	1,491	1,565	1,644	1,726	1,812	1,903	1,998
2	Volume (units)	98,146	94,371	95,442	95,644	96,223	96,223	96,223	96,223	96,223	96,223	96,223
3	Selling Price/unit (£) (1÷2)	12.75	13.39	14.06	14.76	15.50	16.27	17.09	17.94	18.84	19.78	20.77
4	Direct cost of labour (£'000's)	380	380	384	400	419	431	444	457	471	485	500
5	Direct cost of material (£'000's)	328	331	352	352	372	383	394	406	418	431	444
6	Other direct Costs (£'000's)	0	0	0	0	0	0	0	0	0	0	0
7	Total direct Costs (£'000's) (4+5+6)	708	711	736	753	791	814	839	864	890	916	944
8	Contribution (£'000's) (1-7)	543	552	606	659	700	751	804	862	922	986	1,053
9	Overheads (£'000's)											
10	Profit (£'000's) (8-9)											

Good business isn't rocket science

Table 24.   Example from Everyorg Ltd of product / service Low Forecast   Item C

Product/Service: ....Item C...Low Forecast

	Planning Year	-5	-4	-3	-2	-1	Current year	1	2	3	4	5
	Calendar Year											
1	Sales Revenue (£'000's)	428	464	505	558	616	641	666	693	721	750	781
2	Volume (units)	46,762	47,851	49,102	51,236	53,344	53,877	54,416	54,960	55,510	56,065	56,626
3	Selling Price/unit (£) (1÷2)	9.15	9.70	10.28	10.90	11.55	11.90	12.26	12.62	13.00	13.39	13.79
4	Direct cost of labour (£'000's)	175	186	199	216	234	242	252	262	273	284	295
5	Direct cost of material (£'000's)	111	119	128	140	153	159	165	172	179	186	193
6	Other direct Costs (£'000's)	0	0	0	0	0	0	0	0	0	0	0
7	Total direct Costs (£'000's) (4+5+6)	285	305	327	356	387	401	418	435	452	470	489
8	Contribution (£'000's) (1-7)	143	159	178	202	229	239	248	258	269	279	291
9	Overheads (£'000's)											
10	Profit (£'000's) (8-9)											

40

Table 25.   Example from Everyorg Ltd of product / service Low Forecast   Item D

Product/Service: ....Item D......Low Forecast

	Planning Year	-5	-4	-3	-2	-1	Current year	1	2	3	4	5
	Calendar Year											
1	Sales Revenue (£'000's)	1,547	1,672	2,669	2,946	3,201	3,330	3,464	3,603	3,749	3,900	4,057
2	Volume (units)	312,456	318,564	479,826	499,627	512,234	517,356	522,530	527,755	533,033	538,363	543,747
3	Selling Price/unit (£) (1÷2)	4.95	5.25	5.56	5.90	6.25	6.44	6.63	6.83	7.03	7.24	7.46
4	Direct cost of labour (£'000's)	709	752	1,178	1,276	1,360	1,415	1,472	1,531	1,593	1,657	1,724
5	Direct cost of material (£'000's)	412	442	698	764	822	854	889	925	962	1,001	1,041
6	Other direct Costs (£'000's)	0	0	0	0	0	0	0	0	0	0	0
7	Total direct Costs (£'000's) (4+5+6)	1,121	1,194	1,876	2,040	2,182	2,270	2,361	2,456	2,555	2,658	2,765
8	Contribution (£'000's) (1-7)	426	478	793	906	1,019	1,060	1,102	1,147	1,193	1,241	1,291
9	Overheads (£'000's)											
10	Profit (£'000's) (8-9)											

Good business isn't rocket science

Table 26. Example from Everyorg Ltd of product / service Low Forecast Summary
Product/Service: ....Low Forecast

	Product / service	£'000's	-5	-4	-3	-2	-1	Current year	1	2	3	4	5
		Turnover	5,696	5,867	7,529	8,245	8,989	9,330	9,685	10,053	10,437	10,835	11,249
1	Item A	Contribution	701	714	1,019	1,156	1,281	1,513	1,578	1,644	1,649	1,719	1,791
2	Item B	Contribution	543	552	606	659	700	751	804	862	922	986	1,053
3	Item C	Contribution	143	159	178	202	229	239	248	258	269	279	291
4	Item D	Contribution	426	478	793	906	1,019	1,060	1,102	1,147	1,193	1,241	1,291
5	Other items	Contribution	81	89	103	116	131	136	139	144	148	154	158
6		Total/year	1,894	1,994	2,753	3,153	3,589	3,700	3,874	4,057	4,184	4,381	4,587
7		Overheads (including fixed labour)	1,293	1,307	1,430	1,511	1,516	1,577	1,640	1,706	1,774	1,845	1,919
8		Net Profit	600	687	1,323	1,642	2,073	2,122	2,234	2,351	2,410	2,536	2,668
9		Net Profit %	11	12	18	20	23	23	23	23	23	23	24

Good business isn't rocket science

Table 27. Your organisation's product/service Low Forecast

Now, once again, fill in the table with your own information. Work on the items, products or services you have decided on in Table 14 and then provide copies of this form for each and enter your own information as we have done in the Everyorg Ltd examples on the previous pages, summarising your information in Table 28.

Product/Service: ....Low Forecast

	Planning Year	-5	-4	-3	-2	-1	Current year	1	2	3	4	5
	Calendar Year											
1	Sales Revenue (£'000's)											
2	Volume (units)											
3	Selling Price/unit (£) (1÷2)											
4	Direct cost of labour (£'000's)											
5	Direct cost of material (£'000's)											
6	Other direct Costs (£'000's)											
7	Total direct Costs (£'000's) (4+5+6)											
8	Contribution (£'000's) (1-7)											
9	Overheads (£'000's)											
10	Profit (£'000's) (8-9)											

Good business isn't rocket science

Table 28. Your organisation's product/service Low Forecast summary
Product/Service: ....Low Forecast

	Planning Year		-5	-4	-3	-2	-1	Current year	1	2	3	4	5
	Calendar Year												
	Product / service	£'000's											
		Turnover											
1	Item A	Contribution											
2	Item B	Contribution											
3	Item C	Contribution											
4	Item D	Contribution											
5	Other items	Contribution											
6		Total/year											
7		Overheads (including fixed labour)											
8		Net Profit											
9		Net Profit %											

44

2. Developing and summarising the High Forecasts

This is the opposite of the pessimistic forecast and relates to the positive points that have come from your future analysis.

The High Forecast pages follow those of the low forecast ones as follows:

Table 29.   Everyorg Ltd's High Forecast of Item A

Table 30.   Everyorg Ltd's High Forecast of Item B

Table 31.   Everyorg Ltd's High Forecast of Item C

Table 32.   Everyorg Ltd's High Forecast of Item D

Table 33.   Everyorg Ltd's High Forecast Summary.

Table 34.   for your own High Forecast figures (as many as you need), and

Table 35.   for your High Forecast Summary.

Make sure you put in some notes that explain your reasoning. It's easy to forget why you decided on a particular view at a certain time!

Good business isn't rocket science

Table 29.   Example from Everyorg Ltd of product / service High Forecast   Item A

Product/Service: ....Item A......High Forecast

	Planning Year	-5	-4	-3	-2	-1	Current year	1	2	3	4	5
	Calendar Year											
1	Sales Revenue (£'000's)	2,124	2,111	2,617	2,912	3,169	3,590	3,996	4,448	4,950	5,510	6,133
2	Volume (units)	187,256	175,643	205,414	215,613	221,357	236,625	248,456	260,879	273,923	287,619	302,000
3	Selling Price/unit (£) (1÷2)	11.34	12.02	12.74	13.51	14.32	15.18	16.09	17.05	18.07	19.16	20.31
4	Direct cost of labour (£'000's)	513	501	498	543	580	613	663	718	776	839	908
5	Direct cost of material (£'000's)	910	896	1,101	1,213	1,308	1,267	1,331	1,397	1,541	1,618	1,699
6	Other direct Costs (£'000's)	0	0	0	0	0	0	0	0	0	0	0
7	Total direct Costs (£'000's) (4+5+6)	1,423	1,397	1,598	1,756	1,888	1,881	1,995	2,115	2,317	2,458	2,607
8	Contribution (£'000's) (1-7)	701	714	1,019	1,156	1,281	1,709	2,001	2,332	2,633	3,052	3,525
9	Overheads (£'000's)											
10	Profit (£'000's) (8-9)											

Good business isn't rocket science

Table 30.   Example from Everyorg Ltd of product / service High Forecast   Item B

Product/Service: ....Item B...High Forecast

	Planning Year	-5	-4	-3	-2	-1	Current year	1	2	3	4	5
	Calendar Year											
1	Sales Revenue (£'000's)	1,251	1,263	1,342	1,412	1,491	1,628	1,777	1,940	2,118	2,313	2,525
2	Volume (units)	98,146	94,371	95,442	95,644	96,223	101,996	108,116	114,603	121,479	128,768	136,494
3	Selling Price/unit (£) (1÷2)	12.75	13.39	14.06	14.76	15.50	15.96	16.44	16.93	17.44	17.97	18.51
4	Direct cost of labour (£'000's)	380	380	384	400	419	457	499	545	595	649	709
5	Direct cost of material (£'000's)	328	331	352	352	372	402	434	470	508	549	594
6	Other direct Costs (£'000's)	0	0	0	0	0	0	0	0	0	0	0
7	Total direct Costs (£'000's) (4+5+6)	708	711	736	753	791	859	934	1,015	1,103	1,199	1,303
8	Contribution (£'000's) (1-7)	543	552	606	659	700	768	843	925	1,015	1,113	1,222
9	Overheads (£'000's)											
10	Profit (£'000's) (8-9)											

Good business isn't rocket science

Table 31.   Example from Everyorg Ltd of product / service High Forecast   Item C

Product/Service: ....Item C...High Forecast

	Planning Year	-5	-4	-3	-2	-1	Current year	1	2	3	4	5
	Calendar Year											
1	Sales Revenue (£'000's)	428	464	505	558	616	685	763	849	945	1,052	1,171
2	Volume (units)	46,762	47,851	49,102	51,236	53,344	56,011	58,812	61,752	64,840	68,082	71,486
3	Selling Price/unit (£) (1÷2)	9.15	9.70	10.28	10.90	11.55	12.24	12.98	13.76	14.58	15.46	16.39
4	Direct cost of labour (£'000's)	175	186	199	216	234	257	283	312	344	380	419
5	Direct cost of material (£'000's)	111	119	128	140	153	168	186	205	226	249	274
6	Other direct Costs (£'000's)	0	0	0	0	0	0	0	0	0	0	0
7	Total direct Costs (£'000's) (4+5+6)	285	305	327	356	387	426	469	517	570	629	693
8	Contribution (£'000's) (1-7)	143	159	178	202	229	259	293	331	374	423	477
9	Overheads (£'000's)											
10	Profit (£'000's) (8-9)											

Good business isn't rocket science

Table 32. Example from Everyorg Ltd of product / service High Forecast   Item D

Product/Service: ....Item D......High Forecast

	Planning Year	-5	-4	-3	-2	-1	Current year	1	2	3	4	5
	Calendar Year											
1	Sales Revenue (£'000's)	1,547	1,672	2,669	2,946	3,201	3,562	3,965	4,413	4,912	5,467	6,085
2	Volume (units)	312,456	318,564	479,826	499,627	512,234	537,846	564,738	592,975	622,624	653,755	686,443
3	Selling Price/unit (£) (1÷2)	4.95	5.25	5.56	5.90	6.25	6.62	7.02	7.44	7.89	8.36	8.86
4	Direct cost of labour (£'000's)	709	752	1,178	1,276	1,360	1,471	1,591	1,720	1,860	2,012	2,176
5	Direct cost of material (£'000's)	412	442	698	764	822	906	951	998	1,101	1,156	1,214
6	Other direct Costs (£'000's)	0	0	0	0	0	0	0	0	0	0	0
7	Total direct Costs (£'000's) (4+5+6)	1,121	1,194	1,876	2,040	2,182	2,377	2,542	2,719	2,962	3,169	3,390
8	Contribution (£'000's) (1-7)	426	478	793	906	1,019	1,185	1,422	1,693	1,949	2,298	2,694
9	Overheads (£'000's)											
10	Profit (£'000's) (8-9)											

Good business isn't rocket science

Table 33. Example from Everyorg Ltd of product / service High Forecast summary
Product/Service: ....High Forecast

	Planning Year		Current year	1	2	3	4	5
	Calendar Year							
	Product / service	**£'000's**	-5	-4	-3	-2	-1						

#	Product / service	£'000's	-5	-4	-3	-2	-1	Current year	1	2	3	4	5
		Turnover	5,696	5,867	7,529	8,245	8,989	9,973	11,065	12,278	13,624	15,119	16,778
1	Item A	Contribution	701	714	1,019	1,156	1,281	1,709	2,001	2,332	2,633	3,052	3,525
2	Item B	Contribution	543	552	606	659	700	768	843	925	1,015	1,113	1,222
3	Item C	Contribution	143	159	178	202	229	259	293	331	374	423	477
4	Item D	Contribution	426	478	793	906	1,019	1,185	1,422	1,693	1,949	2,298	2,694
5	Other items	Contribution	81	89	103	116	131	155	182	212	248	288	334
6		Total/year	1,894	1,994	2,753	3,153	3,589	4,078	4,743	5,496	6,221	7,176	8,253
7		Overheads (including fixed labour)	1,293	1,307	1,430	1,511	1,516	1,581	1,605	1,626	1,684	1,758	1,835
8		Net Profit	600	687	1,323	1,642	2,073	2,497	3,138	3,870	4,537	5,418	6,418
9		Net Profit %	11	12	18	20	23	25	28	32	33	36	38

Good business isn't rocket science

Table 34. Your organisation's product/service High Forecast

Now, once again, fill in the table with your own information. Work on the items, products or services you have decided on in Table 14 and then provide copies of this form for each and enter your own information as we have done in the Everyorg Ltd examples on the previous pages, summarising your information in Table 35.

Product/Service: ....High Forecast

	Planning Year	-5	-4	-3	-2	-1	Current year	1	2	3	4	5
	Calendar Year											
1	Sales Revenue (£'000's)											
2	Volume (units)											
3	Selling Price/unit (£) (1÷2)											
4	Direct cost of labour (£'000's)											
5	Direct cost of material (£'000's)											
6	Other direct Costs (£'000's)											
7	Total direct Costs (£'000's) (4+5+6)											
8	Contribution (£'000's) (1-7)											
9	Overheads (£'000's)											
10	Profit (£'000's) (8-9)											

Good business isn't rocket science

Table 35. Your organisation's product/service High Forecast summary
Organisation: ....
...............High Forecasts

Planning Year		-5	-4	-3	-2	-1	Current year	1	2	3	4	5
Calendar Year												
Product / service	£'000's											
	Turnover											
1 Item A	Contribution											
2 Item B	Contribution											
3 Item C	Contribution											
4 Item D	Contribution											
5 Other items	Contribution											
6	Total/year											
7	Overheads (including fixed labour)											
8	Net Profit											
9	Net Profit %											

52

3. Graphing the forecasts

And this is one we did earlier from our Everyorg example.

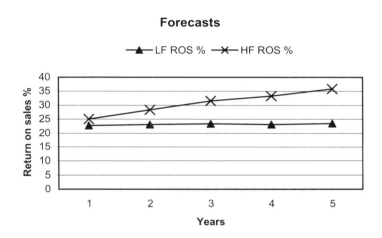

Forecasts

Now it's your turn, have a go!

Table 36. Your organisation's product/service Forecast Graph

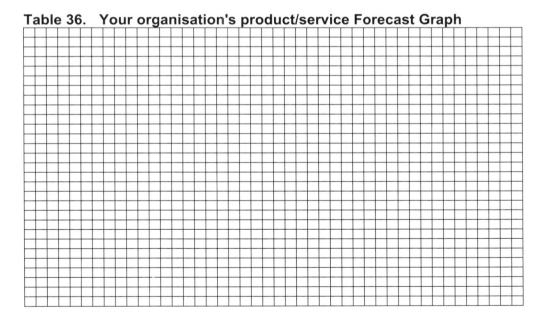

5 *The ugly truth*

Gap analysis

Having created our forecasts we are now going to look at "Gap Analysis". This is simply plotting our Targets (what we want to happen) on the same chart as our Forecasts (what we think will happen) and looking at any "Gaps".

Once again here's our Everyorg example showing Targets and forecasts on the same graph, displaying the 'gaps' or variation of anticipated performance.

Good business isn't rocket science

Graph 3

Steady performance

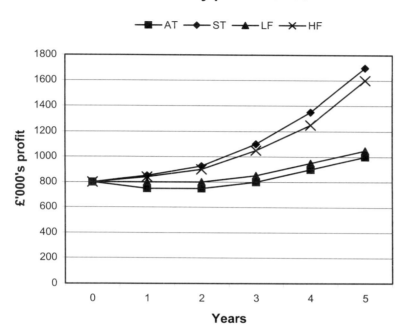

In this example we see a more familiar pattern. Things seem fairly fixed for the next couple of years and after that Low Forecast is above Low Target allowing for a degree of confidence in planning for the future.

This is a frequently found pattern. If everything goes well the organisation will come close to a satisfactory profit on present strategies but even with normal conditions performance will not be too bad. Suggests a steady, sensible strategy.

Good business isn't rocket science

Gap analysis summary

We'll start by looking at an example from Everyorg Ltd and see what implications we can draw from our Targets and Forecasts graph that we've reproduced below.

Everyorg Ltd example of gap analysis summary.

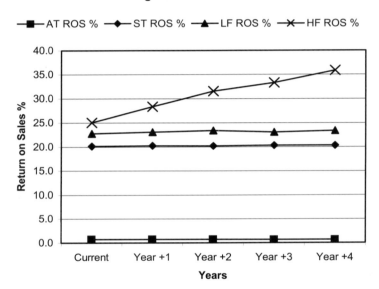

Targets and Forecasts

Viewing the graph we can see that Low Forecast is unusually above Satisfactory Target. This is very unusual but means that we are doing very well indeed or else we need to check our targets again and verify their accuracy!
We know that businesses rarely track on HF but that anything below AT is unacceptable. Since our low forecast is above both of our targets, which we will find acceptable for this example, a more adventurous strategy than we would otherwise be able to promote is considered as realistic.

Good business isn't rocket science

It is hoped that you will now appreciate the usefulness of this exercise. Think carefully about what your graph means for your business and get the objective view of others to confirm or challenge your assumptions. Do not be tempted to stop here and go off to address the situation unless your graph is dire in the extreme. Hold the information you have gathered and feed it into the sections that follow.

Write down the findings of your gap analysis in this box.

The gap analysis findings are:

6 *Know thyself*

Up to now we have focused on producing financial information regarding the past and present and have used this to create a forecast of the future performance of the business. However, forecasts are informed "guesstimates" and you should not therefore base a strategy on these alone. We need to discover some collaborative evidence to support the work we have done so far.

SWOT analysis

The tool we shall use to do this is called SWOT analysis where SWOT is the acronym for Strengths, Weaknesses, Opportunities and Threats. You need to collect information under each of these headings and then do some evaluation of it.

As Table 35 below shows, the Strengths and Weakness relate to the business, they are "internal" factors. The Opportunities and Threats relate to the environment within which the business operates and are "external" factors.

Table 35. SWOT Analysis

	Positive Factors	Negative Factors
Business profile	Strengths	Weaknesses
Environmental scanning	Opportunities	Threats

We will start with the internal issues – Strengths and Weaknesses. Remember that we are looking for "Strategic" issues, so stand back from the minutiae. Look for the major things that have or will effect the success or failure of your business, things that are critical or that you do significantly better or worse than other businesses like yours. Make your thoughts wide ranging across the whole business. This list of issues, which is not by any means exhaustive, will give you some areas to consider:

- strategy,
- finance,
- systems,
- communications,
- people,
- marketing,
- sales,
- customers,
- products/services.

Involve others and have a good brainstorming session to get as comprehensive a list as possible.

Good business isn't rocket science

Be sure to include as wide a range of opinion as possible and do not dismiss those voices that you do not agree with. Avoid clichés such as "loyal workforce" and avoid self-congratulation statements such as "dynamic management". Some statements may mask deeper issues e.g. "poor productivity – weak manufacturing management" or "no new products – no product innovation process", do not be afraid to dig to the root.

Once you have made your analysis of strengths and weaknesses and noted down your findings, its time to move on to the "external" factors – Opportunities and Threats. As with strengths and weaknesses, we are looking for major strategic issues that might critically effect the business in either a positive or negative manner, they are equally important.

A good environmental scanning framework to focus thought is called STEEP analysis which thinks through Societal, Technological, Economic, Environmental and Political issues:

- What is happening in society that might affect your business e.g. the move toward organic produce, working patterns etc.
- What technological changes are on the horizon, perhaps a move from metal components to carbon fibre.
- Is an economic downturn or boom on its way?
- What environmental effects need to be considered with your organisation's products and/or services?
- Political drivers for change in health and safety, equality, competition etc. can seriously affect many businesses.

What are the issues that might affect your business? Once again create a list of headings and work from there, STEEP gives you a good start.

But we haven't finished yet, there are other areas of opportunities and threats that you need to consider. It's a good idea to think through issues using Michael Porter's "Five Forces"

- The threat of new entrants to your markets
- The power of your suppliers
- The power of your customers
- The threat of substitute products or services
- Competition

So lets see how we've got on with Everyorg Ltd.. On the next page you'll see our results and notice how high level and concise they are.

Table 36.   Everyorg Ltd SWOT examples

Strengths

Description
Marketing
Customer service
Quality products

Weaknesses

Description
Some item overheads
Limited amount of product development
Product planning and scheduling
No overseas experience

Opportunities

Description
Overseas operation
New and complementary product development

Threats

Description
New entrants to industry
Over capacity
Foreign competition

Ok, away you go. Use Tables 37 – 40 on the following pages to record your S.W.O.T analysis.

Table 37. Strengths

Description

Table 38. Weaknesses

Description

Table 39.   Opportunities

Description

Table 40.   Threats

Description

SWOT summary

You should now have a list of Strengths, Weaknesses, Opportunities and Threats. It should not be a huge list, probably no more than half a dozen items under each heading. Remember that these issues are the most significant ones that concern your organisation.

Now we are going to use the classification column and conduct an analysis that will give some priority to the issues that we have determined under the four SWOT headings.

Strengths and Weaknesses

Lets start with the ranking of Strengths and Weaknesses. Each should be ranked according to the following table and given the Classification S, T or O.

Table 41. Strengths and weaknesses assessment

Class	Level of importance	Level at which to be dealt with in the organisation	Parts of the organisation that are affected	Executive responsibility
S (Strategic)	*critically important*	to be considered in strategy development	Mainly affects the whole organisation	Handled by Board or senior management team
T (Tactical)	*important*	to be addressed in normal improvement project plans	Usually affects one or more departments, products/services etc	Effected by managers and/or project teams etc.
O (Operational)	*operational*	to be dealt with on an ad-hoc or everyday basis	Affects individuals, operations, specific processes, etc	Usually effected by managers and/ or supervisors

So, go through your Strengths and Weaknesses and allocate an S, T or O to each one based on the above classification. You need to be very critical when doing this. If you are not, you may end up with all of the issues being strategic ones. Be very critical, you should end up with only one or two really critical ones unless your organisation is out of control!
You need to be really decisive here!

Opportunities and Threats

To prioritise opportunities and threats we look at two factors for each issue identified, the impact on the organisation if something happened and the likelihood of it happening.

IMPACT			LIKELIHOOD	
Ranking	Score		Ranking	Score
High	3		High	3
Medium	2		Medium	2
Low	1		Low	1

We take each **opportunity and threat** and decide whether the impact level will be high, medium or low on the organisation. Then we do the same for the *likelihood of it happening* and eventually arrive at a scoring classification for each opportunity and threat by multiplying the scores for each ranking. This classification is then interpreted as follows:

Table 42.   Opportunities and threats assessment

Ranking	Level of importance	Level at which to be dealt with in the organisation	Parts of the organisation that are affected	Executive responsibility
>=6 (greater than or equal to 6)	*critically important*	to be considered in strategy development	Mainly affects the whole organisation	Handled by Board or senior management team
>=3, **<=6** (greater than or equal to 3 and less than or equal to 6)	*potentially important*	to be addressed in contingency plans after lower risk has been established. Such a risk may easily be dealt with at operational level.	Usually has an effect on one or more departments, products/services etc	Dealt with by managers and/or project teams etc.
<=2 (equal to or less than 2)	*No strategic risk*	May be dealt with at a later stage	Affects individuals, operations, specific processes, etc	Usually effected by managers and/ or supervisors

So by applying these sets of conditions we get some degree of priority into the internal and external SWOT issues.

Let's have a look at Everyorg again and see what its SWOT outcomes are.

Table 42. Everyorg Ltd example SWOT summary

Internal criteria

Strengths	Class	Comments
Marketing	T	Already functioning well but needs to be maintained
Customer service	T	Functioning well, regarded as critical success factor (CSF)
Quality products/services	S	Another CSF but level determined by strategic review

Weaknesses	Class	
Some item overheads	T	Long term efficiency plans to be considered with projects as part of action plans
Limited amount of product development	S	Profile needs to be raised to match reputation of quality outputs (items)
Product planning and scheduling	T	Greater efficiencies to internally match and reflect level of customer service
No overseas experience	T	This may become a strategic issue in the next few years but at present there is a need to closely monitor overseas enquiries and their outcomes.

External criteria

Opportunities	Score			Comments
	I	L	Tot	
Overseas operation	3	3	9	Background work needs to be done within the next year to determine the organisational implications of trading overseas. It will have a high strategic impact and probability.
New and complementary product development	3	2	6	Market is beginning to demand more choice and so it is necessary to investigate opportunities at strategic level.
Threats				
New entrants to industry	3	1	3	Possible high impact but low probability owing to large amount of capital required
Over capacity	2	1	2	Some impact but the likelihood is low as the order situation is buoyant and is forecast to be so for some time
Foreign competition	2	2	4	Large foreign conglomerates would have the power but not the domestic expertise, unless it was bought in and so the impact and likelihood are medium probabilities.

Now its your turn to use Table 43 to rank your SWOT analysis.

Table 43. SWOT Summary

Strengths	Class	Comments
Weaknesses	Class	

External criteria

Opportunities	Score			Comments
	I	L	Tot	
Threats				

In the next chapter we are going to start putting all this information together, so hold tight!

7   A fork in the road?

You have now gathered a lot of information about the business and refined it into the two targets and two forecasts comprising the Gap analysis, and into the SWOT analysis. Now we have come to that place on the journey where we need to pull it all together, decide what it means, and decide which way to go in the future. Is there a fork in the road or is there a straight path ahead. Let's find out.

To do this from the work we've already done we need to analyse certain information and then develop it to eventually arrive at our organisational strategies. We will do this in the following manner:

1. **Develop key issues** relating to the organisation.
2. **Generate strategic options** from these key issues (develop alternatives of what we need to do to meet our key issues).
3. **Select the strategies** (the preferred strategic options will become our strategies) that we need to further the organisation's progress.

And now let's take one at a time.

7.1 Develop key issues

We start by comparing the Gap and SWOT analyses. To see how we do this we will work through the Gap and SWOT examples from Everyorg Limited.

We'll start by looking at the Gap analysis and then going on to the SWOT. We've reproduced the Gaps graph and comments again for you to have them handy.

Gap Analysis

Targets and Forecasts

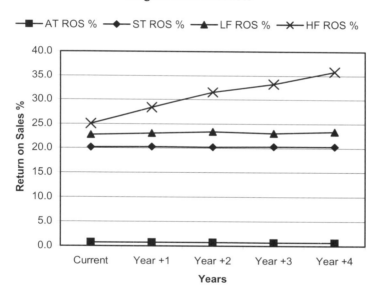

Viewing the graph we can see that Low Forecast is unusually above Satisfactory Target. This is very unusual but means that we are doing very well indeed or else we need to check our targets again and verify their accuracy!
We also know that businesses rarely track on HF but that anything below AT is unacceptable. Since our low forecast is above both of our targets, which we will find acceptable for this example, a more adventurous strategy than we would otherwise be able to promote is considered as realistic.

Domestic market conditions appear to be reasonably stable for the sales of our items and this situation will give us time to plan and overcome our weaknesses and threats. Altogether the picture points to a fairly adventurous strategy that needs to be tempered by our weaknesses and potential threats.

So, how does this relate to our SWOT analysis?

Let's have another look and find out.

SWOT analysis

Everyorg example SWOT summary

Internal criteria

Strengths	Class	Comments
Marketing	T	Already functioning well but needs to be maintained
Customer service	T	Functioning well, regarded as critical success factor (CSF)
Quality products/services	S	Another CSF but level determined by strategic review
Weaknesses	**Class**	
Some item overheads	T	Long term efficiency plans to be considered with projects as part of action plans
Limited amount of product development	S	Profile needs to be raised to match reputation of quality outputs (items)
Product planning and scheduling	T	Greater efficiencies to internally match and reflect level of customer service
No overseas experience	T	This may become a strategic issue in the next few years but at present there is a need to closely monitor overseas enquiries and their outcomes.

Good business isn't rocket science

External criteria

Opportunities	Score			Comments
	I	L	Tot	
Overseas operation	3	3	9	Background work needs to be done within the next year to determine the organisational implications of trading overseas. It will have a high strategic impact and probability.
New and complementary product development	3	2	6	Market is beginning to demand more choice and so it is necessary to investigate opportunities at strategic level.
Threats				
New entrants to industry	3	1	3	Possible high impact but low probability owing to large amount of capital required
Over capacity	2	1	2	Some impact but the likelihood is low as the order situation is buoyant and is forecast to be so for some time
Foreign competition	2	2	4	Large foreign conglomerates would have the power but not the domestic expertise, unless it was bought in and so the impact and likelihood are medium probabilities.

In the example of Everyorg's SWOT analysis above we see that there are seven negative issues (weaknesses and threats) and five positive issues (strengths and opportunities) indicating that, overall, we need to apply some form of improvement measures to our organisation's operations. This may not always be at strategic level but it does provide an indication of the balance of our activities that we should consider when we have analysed the effect of ranking.

Lets look at the ranking scenario and see what it tells us.

The main issues that SWOT highlights for strategic attention are those with the highest ranking:

On the positive side:
- Quality products/services
- Overseas operation
- New and complementary product development

On the negative side:
- Limited amount of product development

These are all the issues given a Class 'S' and/or those given a score of >=6)

We need to consider these as part of our total approach with the Gap analysis and so we use the next table to begin our strategic summary.

Table 44. Example of a strategic summary sheet

Strengths outweigh weaknesses	Strengths and weakness equal	Weaknesses outweigh strengths
Opportunities outweigh threats	Opportunities and threats equal	Threats outweigh opportunities
Circle the above box that applies and write comments here:		
From SWOT analysis strategy should be adventurous	From SWOT analysis strategy should be defensive	
Circle the above box that applies and write comments here:		
From Gap analysis strategy should be adventurous	From Gap analysis strategy should be defensive	
Circle the above box that applies and write comments here:		
Repeated common themes:		
Key issues to be addressed: 1.　　　　　　2.　　　　　　3.　　　　　　4.		

Now we'll use this table with the Everyorg Ltd example.

Good business isn't rocket science

In Table 45, Everyorg's comments and answers are in italic.

Table 45. Everyorg Limited's strategic summary sheet

Strengths outweigh weaknesses	Strengths and weakness equal	⬭ Weaknesses outweigh strengths ⬭
Opportunities outweigh threats	Opportunities and threats equal	⬭ Threats outweigh opportunities ⬭

Circle the above box that applies and write comments here:

We have more weaknesses and threats than strengths and opportunities.

⬭ From SWOT analysis strategy should be adventurous ⬭	From SWOT analysis strategy should be defensive

Circle the above box that applies and write comments here:

Very profitable in spite of weaknesses and threats. Confidence in Customer service marketing and quality gives a steady positive forecast that will allow some experimentation. Therefore a degree of adventure may be built into our strategy.

⬭ From Gap analysis strategy should be adventurous ⬭	From Gap analysis strategy should be defensive

Circle the above box that applies and write comments here:

Forecasting good profits for the foreseeable future and some degree of experimentation may be incorporated into the strategy.

Repeated common themes:

product development

Key issues to be addressed:

1. *Increasing new and complementary quality product/service development*
2. *Resources to commit to investigate overseas operation*

You will be able to see from this example how the various strings have been pulled together to arrive at what appears to be very positive key strategic issues.
Now it's your turn again in Table 46.

Table 46.   Strategic summary sheet

Fill in this table, with your own examples, as shown above.

Strengths outweigh weaknesses	Strengths and weakness equal	Weaknesses outweigh strengths
Opportunities outweigh threats	Opportunities and threats equal	Threats outweigh opportunities
Circle the above box that applies and write comments here:		
From SWOT analysis strategy should be adventurous		From SWOT analysis strategy should be defensive
Circle the above box that applies and write comments here:		
From Gap analysis strategy should be adventurous		From Gap analysis strategy should be defensive
Circle the above box that applies and write comments here:		
Repeated common themes:		
Key issues to be addressed: 1. 2. 3. 4.		

You should now have identified the key or "strategic" issues and challenges that face your business. Throughout the process so far you should have been including input from many sources and people. Now is a good time to go back to appropriate people and double check your analysis and the thinking and reasoning behind it.

7.2 Generate strategic options

Once you are confident that you have the key issues, it's time to identify the way forward.

- What are the options?

- What do we need to do to ensure that the key issues are met?

The first stage in doing this is to work through the key issues and develop ways of addressing them that we call 'strategic options'. Table 48 has been designed to help you do this but before you start work on it have a look below in the example table.

Table 47. Strategy generation example

Everyorg Limited

Key Issues	Strategic Options
1. Increasing new and complementary quality product/service development	a. Restructure present research and development to deliver new and complementary products/services at the desired quality level. b. Focus on new products to supersede present ones without upgrading. c. Concentrate on upgrading only as it is quicker to point of sale than new products.
2. Resources to commit to investigate overseas operation	a. Conduct operation/project to qualify overseas marketplaces and opportunities. b. Undertake research on overseas competitors products.

The above example should have given you a push in the right direction. We've only written two or three strategic options to give you a flavour of what to do but in your own examples you must try to put down as many as possible. Now try to complete Table 48 for your own business and generate a number of alternatives. However, sometimes there may be only one course of action – but that is rare.

Good business isn't rocket science

Table 48. Strategy Generation

Key Issue	Strategic Options

7.3 Select initial strategies

Now that we have created some strategic options we need to evaluate them. To do this we ask questions of each option. If there is only one emerging strategic option we ask the same questions of that.

1. Will it prevent us dropping below AT?

2. Does it build on the strengths classed "S"?

3. Does it correct or neutralise weaknesses classed "S"?

4. Is the impact of threats scored >=6 reduced?

5. Is there exploitation of >=6 scored opportunities?

Use the form in Table 50 on page 88 to make this analysis. Give each option either a plus point for each 'yes' or a minus point for each 'no' answer, then total them up.

The options with the highest scores are your strongest candidates for future success. These should now be discussed with a wider group and preferably an objective outsider. You need to be confident that the options you are choosing from are realistic, valid, affordable, and have a strong chance of success. Unless there is only a single option, the final choices are personal ones. Even if there is only one option it must fulfil most of the criteria in the questions above. If not, you must go back to the drawing board, perhaps draw on a wider group/different of advisors. In the end the strategic options you choose must address the issues you have identified!

When you have identified your group of (or single) strategic options, they may now be termed 'strategies' and it's time to evaluate them and work toward the implementation plan.

Once again we have an Everyorg Ltd example on the next page before you try your hand in Table 50.

Table 49.   Everyorg Limited Example of strategic option qualification

Strategic Option	Will it prevent us dropping below AT?		Does it build on the strengths ranked "S"?		Does it correct or neutralise weaknesses ranked "S"		Is the highest impact of threats reduced?		Is there exploitation of the highest ranked opportunities?		Scores		Overall Total
	Yes	No	Yes	No	Yes	No	Yes	No	Yes	No	Yes	No	
1. Restructure present research and development to deliver new and complementary products/services at the desired quality level.	+1		+1		+1		+1		+1		+5		+5
2. Focus on new products to supersede present ones without upgrading.		-1	+1		+1			-1	+1		+3	-2	+1
3. Concentrate on upgrading only as it is quicker to point of sale than new products.		-1	+1		+1			-1	+1		+3	-2	+1
4. Conduct operation/project to qualify overseas marketplaces and opportunities		-1	+1			-1		-1	+1		+2	-3	-1
5. Undertake research on overseas competitors products		-1		-1	+1		+1		+1		+3	-2	+1

Good business isn't rocket science

Table 50.   Strategic option qualification.

Give each option either a plus point for each 'yes' or a minus point for each 'no' answer, then total them up.

Strategic Option	Will it prevent us dropping below AT?		Does it build on the strengths ranked "A"?		Does it correct or neutralise weaknesses ranked "A"		Is the impact of threats ranked "H" reduced?		Is there exploitation of "H" ranked opportunities		Scores		Overall Total
	Yes	No	Yes	No	Yes	No	Yes	No	Yes	No	Yes	No	

8 How good is that then?

Let's now evaluate your strategies in the light of some established wisdom and a few examples. To help us do this we refer to the criteria found under the two sub-headings of common generic strategies as explained in the following text.

Common Generic Strategies

Having identified your strategies, it may be useful to identify a measure of them by a comparison exercise. The following are "common generic strategies" that can be used as a "best fit" description for your overall strategic direction. Which one applies to you? Common generic strategies are found under the two main headings, "Proven" and " Hazardous" as shown below:

Proven strategies

- Specialisation
- Customer perceived added value
- Improved productivity

Hazardous strategies

- Price leadership
- Growth
- Diversification
- High Gearing

Which best describes your overall strategic situation?
Before selecting a particular strategic direction you should be aware of the potential problems and/or benefits of these generic studies. We will now look at each one individually.

Proven strategies

Specialisation
Specialisation is the strategy of specialising in a particular area. The idea is to be "good at one thing rather than mediocre at many" or to "excel at what you do well, get rid of the rest!"

As with most strategies there are potential benefits and/or problems. The possible benefits of specialisation are: a focused use of limited resources; you are able to exploit market segments; and it could result in a strong market presence.

The problems of specialisation are: there may be a lack of market relevance in some segments; and it could lead to obsolescence of products/services or of markets.

Customer perceived added value
Customer perceived added value is the strategy of making your offering 'special'
There are many ways to add value to your product:
- Responsiveness
- Just In Time deliveries
- Difficult jobs
- Technical support
- Exclusivity

For customer perceived added value you need to keep close to the customers needs.

Many organisations find it necessary to change employees' attitudes towards customers and, if this direction is followed, human resource development maybe an essential support strategy.

Improved productivity: Technology lead
The aim of improved productivity by taking a technology lead is to improve the bottom line through improved productivity by introducing new technology.

Good business isn't rocket science

However the problems that you may face with a technological step change are that it is high cost (with which there are many hidden costs); there is a learning curve; you may encounter resistance to the technology; and the technical and commercial risk associated with it.

Many companies turn to technology with high expectations, only to find it does not provide the anticipated productivity and efficiency gains. Indeed, the risks for some businesses of relying on technology <u>alone </u>is very high.

Improved productivity: Process lead
It is also possible to improve productivity via a process lead.

Did you know that 30% of employee's time is wasted dealing with errors or through duplication of effort?

Did you also know that 90% of product lead-time is spent 'on the floor' waiting for machines or waiting to be moved?

There are also the benefits of process management which are: it's low cost; low risk; and there is employee involvement.

Hazardous strategies

Price leadership
Price leadership is fine if you have the purchasing power; economies of scale; the overseas manufacturing capabilities; and the technological leadership.

However it is a different story for the other businesses as they have reduced margins; are more vulnerable; and are at risk of becoming 'sucked' into a downward spiral.

Growth
There are numerous demands if you wish to pursue a strategy of growth. There is the need for increased management energy; overheads will be increased; you will need cash for new assets; and cash for working capital.

You may lose flexibility, will growth increase profit?

Will growth be at the expense of profitability?

Good business isn't rocket science

One company we worked with had the following record:

Year	Turnover	Profit
1990	£1,000,000	£100,000
1995	£5,000,000	£5,000

Diversification
Diversification does have its pitfalls. It can lead to dissipation, not only that but a confused market image. It can be argued that this is the opposite of specialisation as you maybe going away from the Company's area of expertise and knowledge. With diversification there is always the high risk of non- acceptance in "new" markets as their may already be established "players" there.

High gearing
High gearing usually means that the organisation is borrowing too much money to fund its activities and unless sufficient profit is being made it will not be able to meet its financial commitments.

Now list your own strategic options in the table on the next page and see how they may be termed and qualified.

Good business isn't rocket science

Table 51.   Everyorg Ltd's example of determining strategic direction and potential risk.

Strategies	Corresponding Generic strategy	Risk element(s)	Acceptability comments
1. Restructure present research and development to deliver new and complementary products/services at the desired quality level.	Proven: Productivity	Time to deliver and costs	Several main variables need to be overcome - mainly staff and quality level - but completion will provide the professional approach we lack in this area
2. Focus on new products to supersede present ones without upgrading.	Proven: Added value	Customer demand	Needs qualification for direction but then very positive
3. Concentrate on upgrading only as it is quicker to point of sale than new products.	Proven: Productivity	Customer demand	Needs qualification for direction but then very positive
4. Conduct operation/project to qualify overseas marketplaces and opportunities	Part of growth scenario but little risk apart from those shown	Timescale and cost	Needs to be undertaken if we're serious - must determine timescale and cost are satisfactory
5. Undertake research on overseas competitors products	Part of growth scenario but little risk apart from those shown	Timescale and cost	Needs to be undertaken if we're serious - must determine timescale and cost are satisfactory

Good business isn't rocket science

Table 52. To help determine strategic direction and potential risk.

Strategies	Corresponding Generic strategy	Risk element	Acceptability comments

This exercise will give you some insight into the risk involved in your strategic options so that you may further refine them. The outcome of this short exercise should be a prioritised list of the strategies with which you feel most comfortable.

9   Let's do it!

We've gathered lots of data, turned it into information, and developed our strategies. There is a temptation to sit back and admire what we've done and talk endlessly about what we've learnt. However, if we stop now we have achieved nothing! You would be amazed at how many businesses, having gone to all the trouble of developing a strategy, which they fully believe in, then fail to implement it! So let's get on with working out how to implement the strategies that you have just developed for your business.

9.1   Core and supporting strategies

It is important as a business to identify your core and supporting strategies. **Core strategies** are your 'corporate ends', that is, **what** you want the organisation to achieve. **Supporting strategies** are the 'means' to achieve your core strategies and outline **how** you will deliver them. They may become functional ends for action plans or maybe operational issues.

It is important to separate core from supporting strategies. The distinction may seem somewhat abstract but it allows us to refine and develop the strategies into eventual actions.

We've actually already arrived at our core strategies by continually refining our key issues. If you remember, the process we performed on our strategies was to assess them for risk. By doing this we have ended up with those strategies that we have confidence in achieving. Usually there are no more than 4 to 6 of them.

These strategies tell us WHAT we need to do and act as the core strategies for the organisation.

Using them as our base we are going to expand them into supporting strategies. Asking ourselves HOW we are going to achieve the core strategies does this.

So, for each of the core strategies we need to fill in another table as show by the example in Table 53.

Table 53.   Everyorg Ltd example of Core and Supporting strategies

Core Strategy
1.   Restructure present research and development to deliver new and complementary products/services at the desired quality level.
Supporting Strategies a.   Establish the performance criteria (measures) and their levels that we need to bring the present R&D to the desired performance and quality levels. b.   Review the present work and effectiveness of the present R&D departments compared to the new standards. c.   Set out the means to achieve the new standards in the form of an action plan.

9.2 Your business - core and supporting strategies

With that example under your belt it is now your turn. Complete Table 54 by identifying:

- Core strategies
- Supporting strategies

Table 54. Your business core and supporting strategies

Core Strategy
Supporting Strategies

Repeat this process for all your core strategies.

When we have completed this section we like to stand back and look at what we've completed. We do this by taking an overview as shown in the next section.

9.3   Core strategy qualification overview

Now that we're almost there it is prudent that you should consider a strategy qualification overview by using Table 55 (or similar) that follows on the next page to:

- Define the desired outcome of your core strategy (one per table).

- Determine the relevant background concerning this desired outcome.

- Fully understand what resources are needed to achieve this strategy. (These are normally taken from your support strategies). Include a description and estimate of the costs for each resource needed.

    - Physical

    - Human

    - Training

    - Others

- What major assumptions are being made (pessimistic or optimistic).

- What could possibly go wrong.

- What impact would it have.

- What could you do if it did.

- What contingencies will you need to consider if it does.

Once you have completed Table 55 for each of your core strategies you should have a good measure of confidence in your work.

Table 55.   Strategy Overview

Core Strategy
Desired outcome
Relevant Background
Resources (description and estimate of costs) **Physical** **Human** **Training** **Others**
Major Assumptions
What Could Go Wrong ? **What impact would it have?** **What could we do if it did?**

9.4 Review of organisational potential to deliver the supporting strategies

There are many generic strategic enablers, including:

- Information systems
- Process management capability
- Marketing
- People

These usually always impact on one and other and are closely interrelated and variable in their contribution to the strategy.

Strategic enablers

Whatever strategy you choose you will have strategic enablers, the organisational capabilities required, for delivering the supporting strategies e.g.

- IS/IT infrastructures to improve communications
- Skilled workforce to increase quality
- Process management skills to improve manufacturing efficiency

With limited human and financial resources it is important to focus on developing organisational capabilities that are critical for your success.

Strategic enablers analysis

Using Table 56, identify needed strategic enablers. Also identify present capability and rank the gap as follows:

Rank gap	Gap level
A	Critical
B	Important
C	Minor

Good business isn't rocket science

Table 56. Strategic Enabler Analysis

	Core strategy
	Supporting strategy

Generic Enablers	Needed	Existing	Ranking of Gap	Prioritise
Information systems				
Process management capability				
Continuous improvement capability				
Marketing				
People				
Others (please specify)				

You should now have a good idea of how your enablers will contribute to your strategies and enable you to deliver them. You will also know what work will need to be done to the enabler to help it meet the strategy.

9.5   Issues To Be Addressed

- Core strategies
- Supporting strategies
- Supporting strategy projects

So far in the strategic planning process, we have sought to answer two key questions:

Why?

What?

You should now know what is critical for your organisation, and why.

We now need to answer the following questions regarding your core and supporting strategies and strategic enablers so that specific projects are initiated to meet these major issues:

- Who will have responsibility?
- When will it be done?
- How and where will it be done?
- How will success be measured?

This is key for ensuring the best possible result.

To help with this aspect of the process we turn to another form to bring these criteria together. This form is shown as Table 57.

Good business isn't rocket science

Table 57. Everyorg Ltd example of strategy sheet to show details of action plans

1	Core strategy:	Restructure present research and development to deliver new and complementary products/services at the desired quality level.				
No	Supporting strategy	No	Action / Enablers	Measure	Completed by When	Person responsible
a	Establish the performance criteria (measures) and their levels that we need to bring the present R&D to the desired performance and quality levels.	1	Analyse previous projects to determine their overall timescale and quality achieved.			
		2	Set the new standards that we need to achieve.			
		3	Analyse the present structure and work out what changes will be required to meet the new standards.			
b	Review the present work and effectiveness of the present R&D departments compared to the new standards.	1	Analyse current work and quality and produce report.			
		2	Compare the report's findings with the new standards			
		3	Define the shortcomings that we have at present to meet the new standards			
c	Set out the means to achieve the new standards in the form of an action plan.	1	Compare the reports from 1a3 and 1b3 and decide on what needs to happen.			
		2	Produce a plan to achieve the restructuring.			
		3	Get acceptance and approval for the plan and allocate responsibility, measures and a time frame.			
		4	Get the plan actioned and monitored and completed.			

Good business isn't rocket science

For clarity in Table 57, we've left out the details concerning the enablers but you will be able to see how we've pulled together all the parts of the strategic plan. We would normally put these details on a spreadsheet and add extra information such as:

- actual completion date;
- any problems with enablers that need to be resolved before the actions can be completed;
- initials of those responsible if teamwork is involved, etc.

These core strategies and their supporting strategies and details are easy to list down the left side of a spreadsheet with the timescale across the top, usually left to right in date order.

This arrangement gives a good picture for progress meetings and allows an open style of management to monitor the progress. In our experience it produces good results and creates a certain amount of enthusiasm that passes on to any individuals and teams.

10 Congratulations!

Well done!

You have completed a lot of hard work. Despite the various pain barriers you have had to go through, we know you will have found it worthwhile.

You should now know:

- Where you want to be.
  You've established your corporate aim and in the process have raised some important issues that affect your organisation.

- Why you want to be there.
  You have provided sound reasons for establishing your corporate aim. These have stood the test of sound reasoning and have been robust enough to survive. Only when these reasons change should you consider reviewing your corporate aim.

- How you are going to get there.
  You've established your business plan based on sound processes and factual integrity. You have confidence that the issues you are going to tackle in your plan will deliver your corporate aim, improving and strengthening your organisation in the process.

- Who is going to be doing what.
  Your plan has identified who will be doing what and when and so it provides you with a programme of work that you have to manage. Is this where your real management challenge begins?

Good business isn't rocket science

- What you are going to measure to ensure you get there.
  During the development of your plan you have identified the key performance indicators that are necessary for you to run your business and achieve your aim. You will be planning their use quite closely so that you are in control of your new programme of work. You will react to the changes that the indicators will reveal to ensure that your targets are met.

- Why you are using those measures.
  You know that these measures are designed to deliver the information that you need to meet your corporate aim BUT ONLY if you manage them correctly. These measures provide the signposts for your route to success! You have to react to them and move on to the next stage. It is, after all, up to you!

You should now have in your hands a more detailed and more robust strategic plan than 95% of organisations that exist.

Bon voyage!

INDEX